Jennifer Popescu

Broken Publications

Pacific

Northwest

ISBN-10: 0982858728

ISBN-13: 9780982858721

Published by Broken Publications.
www.brokenpublications.com

Photos by David Picard

Cover design and layout: Jennifer-Crystal Johnson
Edited by Jennifer-Crystal Johnson
www.soulvomit.com

Tangible Soul

By Jennifer Popescu

Table of Contents

Acknowledgments

I would like to thank the people I love more than anything- my three beautiful children, Devin, Noah and Karina, my husband, Alex, who changed my life for the better on every level and continues to amaze, irritate, and fulfill me each day, my two sets of awesome parents- Marina and Thomas Neesen, who raised me to be the woman I am today, and Dorina and David Picard, who continue to guide me on life's journey. Dori, you teach me how to be a better person by example every day. Special thanks to David for taking the pictures for the book cover. I'll buy you a pizza when the book comes out! I would also like to thank Valentin Popescu for helping to give me my wonderful husband- job well done! My little sister, Jordan, and my nephew, Cain, are always kept close to my heart, and my life would be much less vibrant without them. I love you, Banana! Special thanks also go out to Greta Kratz and Scarlett Holder, the sisters nature forgot to give me, and Jennifer-Crystal Johnson, who is not only a soul sister but the owner of Broken Publications. I cannot thank you enough for making this dream come true. To my brother-in-law, Victor- thank you for showing me what it's like to have a brother at all, let alone one as awesome and caring as you are.

I am so very lucky to have been able to add to my family with the amazing friends I've made over the years, whose love gives me strength. Thank you James Ackerman III, whose manliness is only surpassed by his charisma, Jonathan Hogan, Charles Holder, Victoria Myers, Timothy McBride, Tazia Earle, Naomi Smith, Bill Walje, Holly Hartranft, Nathaniel Jones; Erin, Shawn, Anna, Caroline, and India Walden (another family I am honored to have!), Chris Koontz, Gabriel Gutierrez, Jennifer Neesen, Michael and Katherine Bitz, Laura Dougherty, Tissa Brassard, Melissa Merwin (my Isa!), Rose Poblete, Andrew Huynh, Shiree' Dennis, Jennifer Martin, and Sarah and Jonathan Grantham- thank you both for loving my NoahBoah as much as I do.

Special thanks to my grandparents, Barbel Hoffman, Dieter Schmidt, Valerie Neesen and Eveline Neesen. Thank you to my many aunts and uncles.

This book is dedicated to the memory of Joseph Scott Parlati and Opa Wilmes- I never met either of you, but I hope I've made you proud.

To anyone I've missed, thank you, thank you, thank you! There is only so much space in the world!

Jennifer Popescu

Blindsided

I fell into you
not even knowing
I was falling at all
and I'm tiptoeing the line
futilely,
for how can you
possibly hope for oxygen
once already drowning
in the deepest ocean?

Things have shifted
irrevocably changed
my mind seared forever
my heart entangled,
inextricably

and I never saw it coming
blindsided by a bullet train

Ugly

lay back,
arms wide
waiting for the
nails to drive,
the wood beneath
slick with
watered-down blood

head back
expose jaw
waiting for the
knife to slip
the muscle beneath
inconspicuously soft
void of redemption

kneel back
eyes wide
waiting for the
stones to fall
jagged bludgeoning
tearing away
reparation through suffering

self-loathing is such an ugly creature

Cauterized

it took a while but
the flames consumed
all the pretty words I wrote
for you
the sweet stanzas I sent
from my heart into
the universe
it is as if they never existed
both a comfort and
and anguish
the ash on my fingertips
wet with tears

A Second Time

I held your back a second time
heard your voice, insistent
"look at me"
and against all better judgment
I did

I grasped your shoulders a second time
arched my back
let you in
not expecting anything for once
except respect

I whimpered your name a second time
exploding, melting, changing together
a reprieve from judgment, pain, ulterior motive
clean, pure passion
is it any wonder I wanted more of the same?

you closed your door a second time
afraid of what magic two bodies can make
when they care for one another
excuses flapping like fish on the pier
for the first time in your life
afraid of losing
yet following your nature all the same

I write about you a second time
and wonder why

Missing

"Have You Seen This Girl?"
stark black type on curling white sheets
pinned hopefully to unlit lamp posts,
the jackets of the children of the night
the windows of passing cars
She's slipped away, soft voice gone silent,
poetry no longer drips from her lips like manna
for the soul,
and making love feels like a dream, a whisper in the wind,
a tendril of clove cigarette smoke, quickly gone
each grasp, each breath fleeting, taken for granted
leaving them hungry for more, always more
the people have collected their beads from the floor,
sparkling reminder of what was once there
washed gold powder from sleek eyelids
a winter world closes in,
all mirrors cracked, faces
unidentifiable
have you seen this girl?

Unraveling

I am a single thread, no longer content
to be a part of something beautiful,
no longer comforted by the splendor of my settings-
I am unraveling and I cannot stop this
these forbidden, heady, and utterly irresistible
temptations -
Falling deeper and deeper, my thread growing,
so that the mural it was a part of, the intricate
cashmere
is a heap of soft, chaotic, twisted, beautiful tatters
My old self lost, fed to the flames of the uncontrollable

The Waiting Game

the minutes,
hours of my life
tick away
sand through my fingers

I feel their loss
and wonder
what they could have
been
might have been

if I had cared
a little more
done a little more

what I might have seen
had my eyes stayed
open

what I might have felt
were I in your arms

Ode to a Shotgun

you lean against the wall
silver and chrome and
beautiful
I know how to fill you up
make you come
alive
you promise a finality
I can almost taste it
cold, and metallic
rust-colored
and clean

maybe you should go

Weak

this dance is almost painful
in its intensity, its longing, its pining
I close my eyes, still seeing
unable to block out what has been engraved
cauterized, the treatment not healing
the wound
wide-eyed, gasping
yearning for something, no energy to snatch it
I lie on my back, almost motionless
quick breaths of pain the only movement
lift me up, love, for I am weak
lift me up, as I cannot bear
the weight of the world any longer

Finally

It is a wonder you do not set afire
Everything your gaze encompasses
That your lips do not engulf my own
With searing pain, rather than scorching bliss
My sardonic shadowed one, perched high
Above the walls of the cities and hearts of the masses -
I hear your call, your whispered promise
And as long as I've walked this twisted, tangling path
I have heard none that can match it, in sensuality,
In raw desire, intuition, compassion, and love…
I have never seen eyes like yours,
Glinting with a strange combination
Of vulnerability and insinuation,
Of yearning and innocent wide-eyed wonder -
The fierce desire to dominate
And in turn give all of yourself in
Sweet supplication
To the fire that ravages us, tears us down
Only to rebuild and make stronger
I take your hand, having found you
And never look back

Elusive

I used to pride myself on my stability
Feet firmly planted on the ground,
Roots running deep and strong and solid
I could be leaned on, clung to, and gave freely of myself
But gods, I am finding myself hard to get close to
Elusive now, the faint scent of the forest
On the caressing breeze,
I am this, this gliding, dancing tumult of passion and laughter and wisdom
I cannot fully be described,
And you reach for me, they reach for me, longing for something to cling to
once more
I cannot help but step lightly just out of range,
not meaning to be cruel, smiling softly -
I step away, and out, and up, can you see me among the stars?
Grown tired of pretending to be pinned down,
Don't be too sure of me, please, spare your heart, I cannot give more than
this
My tree is barren, but listen to the yearning melody of the wind through
the branches,
breathe the spicy scent of the night

It's Almost Too Late

such great heights
from which to jump
the world weighs heavily
on burdened shoulders
so far removed
from any semblance of belonging
loved ones speak
foreign languages, I cannot understand
their eyes accusing, disappointed
what have I done?
what have I become?
I wish I knew
the emptiness vast, unfathomable
in this untouchable state

Despite All Appearances

(heartache)
doesn't listen when you tell yourself
'it doesn't bother me,
he can't touch me,
no one can hurt me'

taking up residence
with or without your approval
despite all appearances
the sadness settles in
the most subtle kind

I shouldn't care, but I do
I shouldn't let this affect me
why does it seem like the choice isn't mine?

Some things can't be unsaid-
just remember
some barbs, once sent - some hurts, once
inflicted, cannot be unsent, undone
some requiems cannot be
unsung

I will remember this.

Prayer to the Earth-Mother

I appeal to you, sweet earth
bright sky, caressing wind
aide me in my cause
for I have come
with my mustard seed,
bare feet, golden sunlight in my hair
and eyes dark with longing
a hole in my heart

bring back to me, sweet earth
I implore you
that which I have lost
my connection to the salty sea
the lushness of your leaves
and the fertility of your earth
my affinity with creatures such as I

I once walked among them
my offspring and kin, intertwined
bring back to me my son,
taken to the cold north
bring back to me my light
my smile
my gentle compassion

bring back to me my bond with you
this I implore you
this is my plea

Ebb, Flow

I suppose when you are
comfortable alone
in the shadows, wallflower
they overtake you so that
you are nonexistent
unnoticed, unwanted

but your scent, that mysterious
intoxicating aura
faded but not gone
draws them when they're desperate
when they're hurting
and as alone as you've always been

they don't know who you are
how your eyes shine with secrets
knowledge they'll never possess
they tear from you your
magnetism, lest
you detach from the shadows
and stand in the light

and in the end you are left
alone once more
and the pain is not so bad
after a while it becomes
a pain that you're used to

Knives

there are knives everywhere, child,
everywhere there are knives
behind a sweet, calming smile
in the arms of family, the falsity of kin
there are knives

fires that build, the ashes are
not rehabilitation
for the char they leave behind
nothing grows in this ash, child
nothing grows but anguish

there is pain everywhere, child,
everywhere there is pain
no sanctuary, no respite
and most wounded is she who wears her heart
as a gift -
most wounded is she who loves blind

there is pain everywhere, so build up your shell
packed hard with the salt
from your tears
deep and red, gleaming and lonely
there is pain child, build up your shell

5 AM

It's 5 AM again,
the night drags on seeming
unending and yet
sunrise is just beyond
the horizon
a metaphor for life

the room in which
I will lay my head is scented
by sighs, by a sheen of sweat
sweet and deep,
my fingernails tap chipped against
the keyboard and I wish
I had a cigarette, single glowing end
to light this dark room

Why these things matter, I know not -
that my bed is scented of incense and forgotten passion
that the dark lacquer has cracked from my fingertips
that smoke rings in the dusky haze would suit my mood

and yet they do
and here I sit

Egg Hatched

and oh! your anger is a flash of light,
face is all angles and planes,
toughness like gleaming, shining scales
wings undulating, stretching, preparing for flight -
but you are not egg hatched my love,
not born of cold blood, warmed by the fire
of your own audacity, no -

come to me, let me soothe you
with soft hands, languorous eyes
I will show you my own fire, for it is
deep within, so deep and still
you can taste it on my tongue (in my blood)
let us break off those scales, perfect
and dazzling prisms,
hide them away like the treasures they are
and then you will be mine, as mine
as blood is mine, heavy and cloying
on the lips
we need no mirror to capture your gaze
through my eyes, no ears to hear
your song in my voice

Embrace of Earth

at times it's easy to wonder if
the quiet earth is perhaps not
a better suited lover, better suited to hear
the ramblings that fall like drops of honey
from my cracked, rasping lips,
to drink in the tears that have diluted me, so
that they are pure and cleansing water
for I have long since used the salt to shock
myself into feeling, for pain is better than nothing
when you have the choice
what pillow the moist earth would make, what blanket the grass
You see, a heart, overcome with writhing, scraping
bleeding agony for so very, impossibly long
ceases to feel much, self-preservation at its finest
these whispers fall on deaf ears, and yet perhaps
the worms and beetles and sweet, damp earth
would listen, would understand, would embrace and assimilate
this burnt-out star, this faded, frail and drained hyacinth
how easy it is to toy with death, akin to
playing with fire on the fingertips, dancing with the heat
and pulling away before it turns to pain
only the foolish and the brave and the spent
do not fear this
and I am not brave, I am not foolish, and perhaps
I am not spent and I'll regenerate
somehow, I will, for I carry within me the seeds
to new life, to new feeling, to inherent joy
still - oh still at times,
it does ease the spirit to lie among the deadened leaves
and imagine myself one with them

Forgiveness is a Bitter Brew

In dreams I wonder, in darkness I watch
and reflect, and forget, and remember
what I would not give, sacrifice to the glowing fire
to shake myself from this black, hazy cloud
ever enveloping
I wonder if you sent it my way
what verses and curses fell from your lips
like oleander oil, like cyanide kisses
to dampen my eyes and heavy my heart
What blackness have you invoked?
For I have an invocation of my own, dearest foe
I stand barefoot, touching my Mother Earth,
the High Priestess, and I invoke Light
I harness the healing, the strength and the fury
call upon a Warden of the wilds, come to me
and guard me as I embark upon my path
I call upon Love and Forgiveness and Growth
and together these Sisters will push back this hex
And the rain will wash away your writing on my wall
It can soothe all scars, cleanse all filth, and put out the fire
If you but let it

Here, take my hand

Duality

I am the woman
Laughing softly behind pale hands,
Scarves and leaves adorning her hair -
Lost in time, lost in the music
And yet when hurt, when led astray,
I am the girl
Silently defiant behind black lips
Swallowing anger, bitter disappointments
Pain lining her eyes like kohl

Meshed

Arms like a haven
Refuge, cheek against
Firm chest -
Heartbeats steady in our ears
A calm pervades
The tiniest fibers of you and I -
Meshed in this way,
Skin against skin,
Souls lost above us in
Time's oldest battle
Even in rest we are aware
Of each breath,
Each trembling caress
Soft,
Languid,
One

The Pulse and the Rhythm

If you tilt your head
You'll hear it -
There, a beat, heat, life,
Thump -
And then again,
It grabs you, sucks you down
Hips entwined with melody,
Like sex this sound
Earthy, dirty, bliss is this
And now it fills your ears so full
You can't remember
Not hearing
And now your body is no longer
Your own
Slave to the music,
The pulse, the rhythm,
one and the same

Ecstatic Anguish

I am falling in love with you
Why do these words eat away
Instead of replenish -
Sting and burn until
I'd do anything to disappear?
Your smile betrays your own desire -
For more than my body, given so freely
And yet I cannot lose myself this way
Not again,
      (maybe never again)
Why do my fingers tremble when
The telephone rings,
When we've spoken so often -
How can I despair in the sound of your voice,
Then bemoan the length at which we speak
Wanting more, desperately more
And yet willing you never to call again?

Why do I press this deeply inside myself
Refusing to lose what must be given,
Allowing the pressure to build,
The tears to remain unshed,
Sitting silently beside you, mysterious eyes
Ringed in so many layers of black
When they should be mirrors, naked?

And why is it the same for you?

Haphazard

Scavenge from you
To fill what I alone cannot -
And maybe by playing god in my own life
(is that even possible?)
I'll force myself to feel
Tears even taste different now-
Less salt than water, strangely bitter-
Stagnant
I am crystal inside, purified and cold
So that snowflakes are
Warm kisses,
Sweet and soft, I can sense them more intensely
Than yours now,
And no matter how much I
Try
(to talk, to look you in the eye)
I just sit, hands in my lap, thoughts
Like poetry, running on,
Fragmenting
How can I expect you to put me back together
If I can't do it myself?
You drive, hand on my knee
I feel it there from so far away
Smile soft, mind racing, heart thumping futile,
Frightened by the new cracks
Facade spider veined, splintered,
Can I trust myself to let myself heal?

Disappointment

God damn it,
not once, but twice!
you say you are ill,
three hours' notice
phone call jarring me from
the stove
(I've been there all day)
three hours' notice after
six hours of work,
and I believe you -
you sound horrible through the wire,
hoarse and feeble and pleading -
you ask if I'm angry
the answer, no, angry is inaccurate
disappointment paramount,
followed by sadness because
even though I'm falling in love
even though you're different than he was -
I still cannot trust you completely
and the doubt eats away
until there is nothing left, save
burned marinara, salty with tears

You Again

Unable to escape from this
barnacle, attention craving being
that is both
my greatest joy, and
deepest regret…

Unable to escape
the guilt invited by admitting
I would have waited
I'm still not ready, doing this anyhow,
and he's suffering for it

FUCK, how I want to just
roll over, pillow muffling your cries!
3:54 AM again,
And GOD how those whimpers of sorrow
Compel the deepest fibers of ME,
to hold you, to soothe away the hurt,
a love no one else
will ever comprehend

Self-Preservation

God I'm
trying to make it seem as if
waiting for your call
isn't even a blip on
the radar -
trying out the whole
"playing it cool" game, except
with you it's so fucking hard
when all I want is to
feel your chin
resting on my head,
your stomach pressing against
my own,
meeting of butterflies
I'm forcing down a strange
acrid-tasting mixture here,
of hope, of nerves, of annoyance at
the silence of the telephone
(at least on my end)
So ready to sever ties and run, before you do
Can't you sense it?
How ready I am to flee?

Suicidal Tendency No. 21

in a hospital of all places -
chafed by
clinical bleach-white sheets,
hair clinging to my neck, forehead
sticky sweat of inactivity
I stand
and look out the great glass windows
night settling over
the earth like indigo gauze
I look down, contemplate,
visualize a free fall
the ecstasy it must be to feel
the wind in your hair, sharply cool
against your body, knowing
it will be the last thing you
ever feel,
the satisfying finality of it all, if only
there was more distance
between where I stand and
where I long to be

alas I am
lacking in bravery
but then they say
it takes more of that
to crawl back into bed
and cry

Used To

How I used to
Crave your breath on my
Skin, bared
And how we used to
Fumble at each other, urgent,
How it used to
Dispel the darkness,
Burning up the superfluous until
There used to
Be us, no one else

But I'm running
Feet not even on the ground
Afraid of when your
Turn comes to flee

Dim eyed, I greet you
Open armed, closed hearted
And nothing's like it
Used to
    be

Entitled to My Fantasy

So what if I can't stop thinking of you,
And so what if my eyes follow you
More closely than they should
Am I not entitled to drink in
Your presence,
To reclaim a bit of what I once was?

And am I not entitled
A reprieve from soiled diapers,
Grubby cheeks, sticky fingers and
Easy tears?

You move like a goddess of old,
Of femininity and completion
The mystical illusion womanhood beguiles with,
Clean floors and satin sheets and
The freedom to roam at will - whereas

I am its reality, all frazzled hair
And stained clothes,
Dark circled eyes and chunky thighs,
Exhaustion replacing sensuality,
Shackled to this stereotype by motherhood

So let me stare, let me yearn, let me pine
For something long lost, never really mine
Let me live through you awhile, until
I come to terms with my circumstance

Fog and Glass

sometimes the fog is so thick, so all-encompassing
only pain can cut through it, only pain brings light
the only alternative to numbness,

entropy, inertia, internal combustion all at once

I could drown in the music
that speaks so poignantly
to every part of me,

that lends to me emotions I have been robbed of -

I could drown

and sometimes the fog turns
to glass, the glass I'm locked behind
and no matter how I try to
reach out, touch the life on the other side -
cold is all I feel on bruised fingertips,
no amount of pummeling, scratching,
fighting can shatter this
and tears just flow down, leave cloudy streaks
smudges
so that I can't see out

this depth is a new one, a new record
a new state of being that nothing can help
an evolution, regression, minimization of soul

you don't know how far you can fall
until you hit the bottom
and just keep falling

Butterflies

The butterflies are dusting,
airing out their domicile
after a long, long absence
I quiver with them
an internal fluttering,
a great mass of winged frenzy

and though they unpack
the necessities
their suitcases are by the door
just in case

Lost Words

Oh my children, my firstborn,
my tangible soul -
You have been laid to rest among
old bills, coupons,
other people's mail
across a mammoth sea of anguish
I am bereft with your loss
riddled with miniscule holes
the places you once called home

Nothing Compares

If air could smolder
the way your eyes do
if the night glittered
as cruelly as your grin
if the soft grass beneath us
held be as firmly as you do
we would set this world alight
and make love in the ashes

Watercolor World

early morning light
leaves the world a watercolor
the pale pinks and blues of sunrise
are bleeding into each other,
washing skin with their gauze,
filtering over the soft unlined face
of a lover
all that is harsh has become sloping,
rounded, a cocoon of nature's making
it is in this languor, this fleeting perfection
that we are reborn each day anew

Untitled

this pain is so great
I do not feel it yet,
not really, not what is coming
I'm waiting for it to crash
over me,
tear it all away, break down
planning the rehabilitation
in my mind, the blueprints
for rebuilding what will surely be lost -
but it keeps rising, growing, rising,
growing...
I am afraid it will never stop
a tsunami powerful enough
to drown the world

Hiding

mediocre prose coupled with
forced poetry -
half-smoked cigarettes and
half-painted nails
blow-dried hair starting
to curl around the edges,
stubborn and defiant in these
smallest of ways
sleek designer jeans with
baby food stains,
vulnerable eyes behind
mirrored sunglasses

Honesty

So much to process,
So much to compute now
there is no longer any
peace -
the last bit headed out
when you came in
I've lost myself again
in you, in us, in all of this
all these things I cannot describe

Simple doesn't always mean
uncomplicated
and right is not always
straightforward
Sometimes selflessness is exactly
the opposite

Poisoned Mind

decisions made that are seemingly
tattooed to my ribs
sundered behind my eyes
so that not even sleep is escape
infiltrating each thought -
they gnaw away at me
I cannot forget, poison of the mind
Ridding myself would mean
flesh ripped from bone, tearing
myself asunder
the last shards of sanity departing as well

I sink further into the well of guilt
that is mine alone,
sickly snow globe I turn over in my hands
a magnet, the pull is too great
wretched conscience dragging the bones
under the surface
nary a ripple to tell my story
not even a breeze to carry my song
the sigh of water overtaking my short-lived elegy
my forgotten lament

Silence Knows

breathe in
   out
     again
There is nothing here but
silence
and silence knows
  all of your secrets
the hidden pains
the secret joys
the light in your eyes
the dark in your heart
silence knows
and becomes you

Self-Sabotage

If I am destined for great things
Epic sonnets,
Destined to fly -
Why have I clipped my own wings,
By handing you the scissors?

If I am destined to burn
To smolder and shine
Why have I dampened my own fire
With wasted, stagnant tears
That in the end mean nothing?

And if I am destined to love
Compassion as my ONLY guide
Why have I lied to myself, sold the fiction
That nothing can break down this wall?
Time to bleed, to purify,

Time to fly once more.

Untitled

There can be fulfillment in all things
Some just aren't so readily
knowable
There can be freedom in domesticity
But it's not as heady
As some would like
There is also a great light in the darkness
And this I embrace unashamed -
Since everything else is
A compromise

Anemone

I dreamed of you last night
Slippery eel, coral toned and
beautiful
You swam gracefully
Turned back flips, deeply asleep
What did you dream of?
I wondered then
What thoughts unknown to us all
Swam behind closed eyelids in tune
To the waves of your tenuous frame?
You were sleek, smelled of
The rawest sort of life-
Slightly sweet and precious
An anemone in the cradling sea
Of my body
A barnacle of pearls, the best kind
The two of us connect in ways
That nothing can truly sever
My blood your blood,
My bones your bones
And my heartbeat the music
To which you danced

Dream of Words

I dream of words, thick fistfuls of them
Tasting elegance like salted caramel
Heather-scent and candlelight
Breathe them in, long gulpfuls of them,
Like a humid summer night
Thick air, a warm blanket
enveloping
Words suffuse every iota of my being,
Catching breath in throats,
I am adrift in them, alliteration
Tripping up my tongue with beauty,
Soliloquy, incandescence,
Sunrise,
Galvanization, lyrics, divinity

Ironic, Right?

I don't want to write poetry about you
Trivialize what we have with
Lacking description and lukewarm metaphor
We share something beyond even words,
Reveling in the richness of silence, the
magic of heartbeats
The sweet song of tenderness no
Psalm could do justice, no sonnet could capture
no ode define

When I

When I close my eyes
and imagine you doing the same
We are together
If only for a moment

When I surrender myself
To your power, your voice
I feel you inside of me
For a fleeting moment

And when I hear your laughter
Warm and precious in my ear,
I laugh with you and know
What is right and what is true

To A Dear Friend

What pain must live behind
That sneer, that smirk
Dignity so precariously perched
On the ability to deflect attacks
With wit

We have all had to sink or swim,
Adapt or go under
And so he's propelled
By verbal barbs, dancing blue eyes,
A suave irreverence for everyone
and everything

I see this and understand

I Am Here

I'm here
Can you hear me?
Feeling my intuition at
It's most subliminal?
Grab me, damn it!
Don't let me slip away
Like everyone else has.
No
Take what you want
Let go of fear!
Open your eyes so
I can do the same
To my heart

Fetal Position

it crests, washes over
there is no escape
pain so intense
my veins burn
and I realize
I have not been
Breathing -

I lie alone
on my beach of
desolation, the
stars jagged holes
they burrow down
sear through me
waves of anguish
tidal forces
pulling me out
to drown

oh god, please
make it stop
make it quick
eyes swollen shut

oh god please
make it stop

You Deserve Each Other

did you run to her, blind?
not noticing when you
hold her
she is not soft as I am,
but sharp and jagged in your arms?

did you grasp for her, bleeding
not caring now if her teeth
were already finding your neck,
ready to suck you dry?
where I only ever gave to you

did you cry to her, screaming?
not minding that her eyes were ice-cold
and already scanning the horizon for
your replacement, the next meal?
when I only ever loved you, listened?

that shadow across the moon tonight
is me,
I have left this Earth behind
my tears the snow on your cheeks
I am now beyond your reach
My heart no longer your home

Lady Despair

despair has come a-calling
and leaded my limbs
so that the downward spiral
is the natural progression
of things

she doesn't knock, I
awake to see her perched
on the corner of the bed
bruised eyes like a
catastrophe, sinister smile

she is an iron maiden,
pulling me ever closer
to her chest, all the while
knives piercing, it is
all I can do to try and pull away
the worst possible thing

she is like drowning,
overtaking, no oxygen left,
fingertips blue, mouth gasping
dragged down by the very gestures
I hoped would make things better
would bring light to the dark

she knows all my secrets
magnifies my imperfections
skews perspective till I
am as monstrous as she
nails itching to scratch
away my traitor's face

Oh Ye of Little Faith

Oh ye of little faith,
watch as the sun sets in your hands.
Watch as the beauty in your life fades,
watch,
Just watch as the castle crumbles and your crown shatters.
Oh ye of little faith,
Could you not have believed more?

The tapestry is unraveling,
The sky howls with wind
It rushes through empty corridors
And is a stark reminder
Of all that was lost
The tapestry is unraveling
And soon you'll no longer see
My pale, sad face

Oh ye of little faith
Can you still hear my siren song?
I lay down in the snow, just for
A moment
You must join me, rest your weary heart
And let your mind's eye go back
To when you trusted in what was true
And good
Let us both go back to when
The sun shone upon us

A Loving Dose of Honesty

She tries to pull magic
from the air with her fingertips,
searching for that elusive goal,
that lofty ideal she'll never
possess;
Eyes wide with longing unfulfilled,
her arms are open, grasping
likening herself to movies,
songs, other people's success,
other people's loves…
anywhere but here

She jumps over the ledge,
waiting for the wings to sprout,
needle sharp on her back,
a pain she's willing to suffer
the better to write requiems about
later
waiting for him to catch her,
to materialize out of thin air,
weak with love for someone he's never
met

Her life is a movie she refuses
to see,
a book with pages burning, her fingers
black with soot

I Hope You Know

I hope you know
the only way you could be free,
the only path to your salvation,
the tarnished key
was hatred

I hope you realize someday that
the only peace I could
lay at your feet,
the only warmth I could offer,
was created by burning
myself in effigy,
Carving from myself, my bones,
To feed the spark of your outrage

The only truth through lies,
the only happiness through anguish…
I muddled the lines, rippled the water,
guided the artist's hand,
poisoned my own blood so that
you could draw in clean air

I nearly killed us both
to save you
and in turn left myself forever
among the walking wounded

Sunken In

Listless, the
curtains drawn,
I don't want to see
the stars tonight-
have no patience for
the unexplainable

Heart accelerating,
slowing
a constant whine,
engine misfiring
the mirror shows a different
face each time

On the surface, the pond
is still, aqueous,
the earthquakes too tiny
to register,
spidery cracks that meld in
different places

I hold my hands to my cheeks
to keep my face together,
eyes dark, unfathomable
drowning in my clothes,
jumping at the merest sigh

No veins left to tap,
flowered bruises from the barest
of touches-
I am violet, indigo, sickly green,
cannibalized so much that
the landscape has not yet been
rediscovered

Vicious Cycle

Funny that, after all
these years,
the faces change,
but the dynamic stays
the same

I, the one who
cannot even recognize herself
in the mirror,
the one who runs away to
protect her children,
the one who
endures the violence herself,
falsely thinking it would
save them

I, the listener,
the one who smiles and nods,
compassion flowing from me to you-
hugging away the heartache,
open mind and open arms,
the one who becomes a door mat,
yes, you can carve away my flesh for
your own use, yes
please peel away all that you find
distasteful in me,
make me more like you, then find
you didn't like the monster you made

I, the one who lays
abandoned, a child's discarded doll

The seasons change,
the earth keeps spinning,
but no matter where I am,
I, the wilting hyacinth,
cannot stop this vicious cycle

Incendiary

Incendiary, the air between
where you end and I
begin
Distraction is a place
I've rarely been driven
And yet it happens so easily
With you

I feel your lips brush mine
From across the room and wonder
At how the spirit fulfills
What the body yearns for
One way or another

It is never enough,
This fire fully expects to
Consume us entirely
And yet I cannot care
In the face of the sweetness
Of burning

Inability to Let Go

A shadow passes under
the door
and lost as I am
in these tangled thoughts,
I cannot tell if it was really
a shadow, or a specter
of the past come to call

My surroundings are as cluttered
as my mind,
hands idle and useless to this tumult,
I seek only the next sweet taste
on my tongue,
only the next sweet distraction to
grasp onto,
so full is my heart of you, even now

An inability to let go,
papers stacked haphazardly,
books make leaning towers here
and there,
full of places I'd rather be,
lives I'd rather live, thoughts
I'd rather explore,
anything to get away from what once was
and yet still litters my mind

My habitat reflects my state,
a darkness over the moon portends ill will
my trembling fingers remember too well
how quickly the tide can turn
if there is not constant stimulation,
chatter bouncing off the empty walls,
then my memories rise up like a storm,
a tidal wave,
the thought clenching my stomach
in a red-hot iron grasp
leaving me doubled over and gasping

Dandelions

I still remember the day I
gifted my mother a grubby fistful
of dandelions, a makeshift bouquet,
my hands milk-stained from weeping stems.

"These aren't flowers," she said,
"but weeds," and tossed them away.

Gazing out across our yard, my
eyes filled with tears,
clumps of dandelions stood like
golden sentries, so bright against the green.
I made chains with them for my hair,
blew their seeds and cast wishes upon them-
picked many of the most 'perfect' specimens
to grace my mother's powder blue vase…

only to find that my treasures
were not only worthless but
somehow sinister,
weeds in flowery dresses,
wolves in sheep's clothing.

Later that day, I watched
my father pull them angrily from the soil,
hacking them away from the lawn
until it was all green, till no trace
was left of that which was undesirable,

a piece of my innocence dumped with them
into the trash.

Painful Delusions

As it turns out, I am a sucker for magic
pulled out of the air with delicate strands,
woven into something beautiful,
something I was missing, something
I never knew I wanted at all

You crafted shapes with your words
that felt like home to me,
brought to light my redeeming qualities:
the way my eyes caught the light when I
smiled at you, the softness I dared not
let anyone else close to,
the way I laid my heart in my hands and
offered it up, a voodoo relic ready for
your pin

Your fingers wove butterflies of magic,
diaphanous and soft, caressing my face
I closed my eyes, dropped my guard, lay
my heavy burden down
I lived in that magic, breathed it in
Perhaps worst of all you dared claim
that you could not create these things without me,
that I was your muse, your puzzle piece,
and if I ever left, the magic would fade,
your eyes would dim, your life would return to
the blackness you thought for so long
was there to stay

Then came the day I met a sister
in the streets, and her eyes mirrored mine,
her gaze was enraptured, her smile soft,
and I saw you in their depths, your magic…
the spell was broken, for it seems
you sent mirrored promises, reflections to
her as well,
and we were both pawns on the chessboard of your pride…
that day the butterflies died, the snow fell,
my heart became a sepulcher for my dreams

Alien Among Us

I am alien to this life,
Unable to adorn myself
In layers of cruelty,
Armor of selfishness
My skin so thin,
Just a single blow
And the blood pools at
My trembling feet

The delicate tracery
Of veins beneath
The beating heart
Fluttering spine,
It is all here, for
Your gawking privilege
Pale and strange
Not of this world

In my mind I change it,
What I see into
What I can deal with
Softening the edges, blurring
The lines, telling myself the
Ache in my bones is
Alright, the pain in my
Heart is bearable

These lies only
Last so long, and
I gaze longingly at
The stars, my home
Wondering when, oh please
When I may take my place
Far away, insulated against
The agonies of this Earth

Soft Hands

I want soft hands,
calloused but gentle,
a lover like a poem
my lips and hips write,
heartbeat keeping quiet time
cadence forged by a language
beyond words

Not My Sacrifice

Unhappiness follows you like a thundercloud
threatening rain on the brightest
parade,
sneaking shadows and cold breezes to remind you
that no matter what you do
you will always be unhappy, you will always
be in hell

until you learn whatever it is

the universe wishes to teach you-

until you take the steps you need to take

I'd tear off pieces of myself to feed
your happiness
but I can't
That sacrifice is yours to make,
that journey out of the shadows and into the sun
can only be completed
alone

I can only give you the wisdom I learned

on my own expedition through the underworld

Beloved Untamed

You are an uncharted wilderness
a river that flings itself down
mountain paths,
the melting snow that brings clear,
sweet water
there are no guidebooks for your soul, my love
and your cliffs are deadly,
etched against the pale blue sky like swords
I tread lightly with you
my footing sure, I cannot let
your beauty trip me up, I cannot stumble
and lose myself in you

The valley below is ripe with
wildflowers, thorny brush, wolves in meadows
taking down sheep with their sharp,
unforgiving grins
I am not a lamb, I cannot be consumed so readily
I am dressed for the elements, dear heart
and perhaps one day
I'll shed these material impediments
and run through your fields naked and unafraid
of falling

Playing With Fire

Sweet kryptonite
kissing you is like
taking a match to the
scrapbook of my life,
watching it burn with a hunger
that is the purest form of madness
captured by this inferno that
is blind to everything
except the roaring flames
hurt me, change me, end me

just don't stop…

just
don't stop kissing me

The Broken Hearts Club

A broken heart is far more
than the sum of its parts
sure there are the pieces one must
pick up,
(once the searing agony recedes)
But more than that is the new topography
left behind,
the scars silver-pink and tender
accidentally beautiful, sore and throbbing with
an almost musical cadence

A broken heart is never true,
shrouding itself safely behind contempt,
fear,
hope

A broken heart loves in a broken way

www.ingramcontent.com/pod-product-compliance
Lightning Source LLC
Chambersburg PA
CBHW062023040426

42447CB00010B/2116